Preludes

Also by Jeremy Hooker

FROM SHEARSMAN BOOKS

Upstate: A North American Journal
Openings: A European Journal
Diary of a Stroke
Ancestral Lines
Word and Stone
The Art of Seeing
Selected Poems 1965–2018
The Release
Addiction: A Love Story

SELECTED VOLUMES FROM OTHER PUBLISHERS

POETRY
Landscape of the Daylight Moon
Soliloquies of a Chalk Giant
Solent Shore
Englishman's Road
A View from the Source
Master of the Leaping Figures
Their Silence a Language (with Lee Grandjean)
Our Lady of Europe
Adamah
Arnolds Wood
The Cut of the Light: Poems 1965–2005
Scattered Light
Under the Quarry Wood
Alive with Sunlight & Shadow (with Aubrey Hooker)

PROSE
Welsh Journal

CRITICISM
Poetry of Place
The Presence of the Past: Essays on Modern British and American Poetry
Writers in a Landscape
Imagining Wales: A View of Modern Welsh Writing in English
Ditch Vision

ARTIST'S FILM
The moment that holds you (with Liz Mathews)

Jeremy Hooker

Preludes

Shearsman Books

First published in the United Kingdom in 2024 by
Shearsman Books Ltd
PO Box 4239
Swindon
SN3 9FN

Shearsman Books Ltd Registered Office
30–31 St. James Place, Mangotsfield, Bristol BS16 9JB
(this address not for correspondence)

www.shearsman.com

ISBN 978-1-84861-953-1

Contents

Ancestors 9
The Bridge (1) 10
The shore at Warsash 11
Latchmore 12
A Good Man 14
A Dreaming 16
1953 20
A Hampshire Estate 21
The Brook 23
Sway Tower 25
For My Brother David 28
Carpenter 30
133a, St Mary's Street 33
Waters of Wight 35
Singing the Needles 36
IoW ferry 38
The Road to Keyhaven 39
Salterns 41
Two Young Women on Milford Beach 43
Uner Hordle Cliffs 45
Wessex Chalkland 47
New Forest Poem 49
The Knightwood Oak 51
Hatchet Pond 52
Ghost of an unwritten poem 53
In praise of the Lymington River 55
Two Brothers
    1) Brother Oswald 58
    2) Brother Nicholas 59

Author and Mariner   60
On a Sunny Day at Hurst Castle   61
A Man of Heyshott   62
A Lost Painting   63
Artist on Chesil Beach   66
Beach Canvas   68
Gull Dying   70
The Bridge (2)   72
Silent Companion   73
Walking in Longleat Woods   75
Revenant   76
Leaf   77

Acknowledgements   78
A note on autobiographical poetry   79

Ancestors

They come towards me,
and I reach back towards them.
It seems we cannot meet,
that the ground between us is dead.
Yet I feel under my feet the soil
they trod on, the worked soil
from which I take a handful
and hold it to my nose, and knead it
with my fingers.
And for a time, this seems enough.
But nothing will suffice;
they are so far away, each
and all in the apparel of a distant age.
Closer, though, I know in myself
another making, a way
with words that takes me back
to a landscape where nothing is foreign.
And in this place, there is a calling of flesh,
a common desire for earth itself,
and for life ensouled in the dailyness of time.
In my features I know a look that was given,
and in my blood a desire that each calls love.

The Bridge (1)

The name speaks what it meant:
Wainsford – you can see
where the horses lumbered
and the laden wagons shook.
Here the stream gathers, pools,
seems to stand still
under the arch, before dashing on,
through shallows into shadow.

A thing made for a purpose,
functional, economic,
not an object meant
to inspire a boy's first poem.

But nothing can stop the flow
once desire enters the world
and imagination, transfixed
by water under the stone arch,
senses in opaque depths
a source, a deeper mystery.

The Shore at Warsash

It was my first shore, and,
as far as I knew, the only one
with a language of shingle
and shells, of flotsam
and bladderwrack.
Wonderful things,
                    smelling of salt,
on the water and in the air.
I would learn to call them
flying boats, MTBs, landing craft
and biplanes – Tiger Moths
that played at falling out of the sky.

Tides brought in debris
we were forbidden to touch
that might explode in our hands.
Small lives and deaths
kept house between stones,
and gulls with black heads
screamed over us or floated on the swell.

If all the world was like this
it was magic, and beautiful
as crabshells, existence gone out of them,
leaving a new form of being.
It was where I fell in love
with shingle and shells
and words that tasted of salt,
constantly renewed by the tide.

Latchmore

At night, in my bedroom,
I would sometimes crouch
with my ear to the floor, listening
for a train in the cutting
that crosses the heath –
Latchmore, moor of corpses.

How dark it must be, unless
a spark ignited gorse by the track,
starting a blaze that signalled
where a train had passed
and stampeding the ponies.

Listening was like a prayer
where I communed with the living
and the dead – strangers passing
on unknown journeys, and the dead
interred in urns like dinosaur eggs
in the breasts of low tumuli.

A tremor brought distances to mind,
the short haul from Brockenhurst
to Sway, and the longer stretch
from Waterloo to Bournemouth.
The faint earth-shaking also
called up the length of time, from
an ancient battle and the world
of urn burial to the present,
where I knelt on the floor, listening.

It was all a passage in the dark,
a vibration, a sound out there
of the life I was beginning to grow into.

A Good Man

To the memory of Mr George Bullard

I would meet him in his dark suit
and black boots striding across the Common
on his way into Lymington to shop
for himself and his disabled wife,
and visit the library, where
he took out *Ulysses*, and was disgusted.
As an officer in the trenches
he had condemned
his men's fucking language,
and at Hyde Park Corner
he had stood up to combat the atheists.

What he perceived in all was God,
as he taught us, a group of boys
in the vestry of St Marks, Sunday
after Sunday, solemn or mischievous lads
that he meant to make young Christians.
What he imparted with his stories
was godliness and sound morality.
What we gave him was respect.
He was a man who inspired awe.
If anyone offended, he would banish them
with a fury that made us all shake
and sit white-faced to listen harder.

A strong swimmer, once, off
the Norfolk coast, he had been caught
in a rip tide and swept away.
Putting himself in the hands of God,

he let himself drift, until, finally,
the tide delivered him to shore.
Sometimes I think of him,
a man trusting himself to the Spirit
that he believed rules the waves.

All my life, he has returned to me,
a figure from another age, but a man
at my back, counselling
a life I am not worthy to lead.

A Dreaming

Pennington Common, c. 1950

1
Boy and dog, sniffing,
pushing in, mapping
a first terrain.

Chat chat
calls one stonechat
to another among the furze

a pipit rounds her nest
and lays four eggs
hidden in the grass

a lizard basking
in a sunny spot
vanishes at a foot fall

newt larvae
in the weedy pond
are growing lungs

fire-blackened stems,
bright yellow flowers, mark
paths that twist and cross

foot print, paw print
hieroglyph
in dust and sand, where

dog and boy push through
draw in the scent of furze
sniff, and seek, and find

2
If they look up, they see
where the Common ends
in a churchyard
with rows of white stones

It is all real, and all a dream
surrounded
by a world inexorably there
damaged, dangerous

but coming into being
unfinished, fresh
as the gorse that flowers
and pops in the sun

3
There are secrets everywhere
each bush a hiding place
each step an adventure
the dog sniffing
a mighty hunter, the boy
pushing in, the bird
on a bush chat-chatting

lizard and newt alive
each in its place
becoming, feeling
into being, all real, distinct
yet soluble – dream
and world in the making
imagined, quick
at the tips of sense

4

At the horizon
the blue dome of a hill
speaks of the sea

ponies chomp-chomping
bring the Forest on their hooves
It is all out there somewhere

the globe they speak of
but now, boy is too far in
dog aquiver senses rabbit

A little white moth
blunders out of dark
into the sun

small brown butterflies
flutter by, grasshoppers
leap at a footfall

boy and dog
noses down to the path
twisting away, move

farther in
too intent to look up
from the moment in which
they sniff, and seek, and find

1953

Suzanna, I was too shy to respond,
but I remember the tickle of your hair
as you let it brush the back of my neck
as my family sat with your family
in front of their rare television set.

If there was colour in the world,
it drained from our eyes
as we peered into the murk,
where winter seemed to be breaking
in flakes of snow on the ceremony.

I was bored, but I recall the touch
of your hair with fondness, and wonder
about the life you might have led
if you hadn't died so young.

A Hampshire Estate

for Tom Durham

1
Explosively
big carp hurled
themselves out of the lake
with a golden splash.

The place settled back.
Tranquillity seemed eternal.

How closely we watched our floats.

2

Yet the place spoke
with other tongues –

speech of Cornwallis
and brother Admirals
of the Napoleonic Wars

words of a slave owner
and masters of salt pans
murderous tongues
of the sweet and the saline

whisper of the ghost
of Cox's bridge, where
a stream from the lake

flows under the road
and a destitute family
camped, dying of diptheria

news, too, of Dragoon
Lieutenant Colonel Hawker
that great sportsman
famous for the slaughter
of thousands of ducks

3

Innocent, and rich
with life, I loved
all that I knew:
the gold carp leaping,
tiny rudd eager to bite,
peaceful days
that promised endlessness.

The Brook

1

Joining and dividing
between fields, between
banks, and under
alder and hazel shadows,
the brook flows, dscending
from forest heath to the sea,
and as it runs it abandons
an old history of mill and weir
and is forever new.

Before I knew it, it was
Tennyson's, in my mother's voice
with mysteries of 'coot and hern',
a brook I learnt to love
as a stream of images, touched
with sadness of all things
that pass, and pass away.

From early until late
it has run through my life,
now glittering, now dark
and always moving,
changing and ever the same,
breaking, but constantly one.

2

I might be a mayfly, dancing
for one summer evening,
or a lamprey, mouth stuck to a stone,
or a minnow or a caddis grub.
In the face of the stream
I might be a boy or a man.
Whatever we may be
the brook looks on, indifferent
with a surface that reflects
and depths that are hidden.

It is where children come to play
and return to wonder, and grow old.
And what they see eludes them
and is always new, with a voice
that murmurs, sounding under
all other voices of the world.
It passes, and is always passing
but does not pass away. Look!
the sun rides a ripple, the water,
flowing out of shadow,
astonishes with fiery light.

Sway Tower

1

Surprisingly, it stands,
this landmark for the Luftwaffe,
this concrete experiment.
The man who designed it
was a spiritualist
who took instruction
from Sir Christopher Wren,
and a philanthropist,
even a socialist,
who employed local men
to build what he meant to be
a mausoleum. And what he left
was a mark that changed
the New Forest for ever:
this gaunt structure,
visible from far,
towering over trees and fields.

2

Peterson was his name,
a judge retired from India
who brought with his design
a touch of Asia to Hampshire,
that some called his Folly,
an exotic object that became native.

3

Native, but also
a thing of myth, fashioned
from an imperial dream,
more a versifier's fancy
than a poet's object, perhaps,
but in any case, a concrete fact,
a thing fingering the clouds
and surely, to those born
to its influence, a friendly sight.

4

As it was to me, and as it is
in memory, as I knock down
conkers from a tree close by
or fish for small speckled trout
in Avon Water, looking up
to see the tower upstream
or revisit in the shadowland
of dream – this giant
not menacing, but simply
standing, with the whole forest
drawn about its ghostly sides.

5

To my father, it was an eyesore.
But to me it was more than
a thing of Portland cement, spoiling
an artist's ideal of natural beauty.
From the mowing grass, where
I lay making my first efforts at poetry,
trying to catch the life around me,
I would look up and see it
far across the fields.
From there, I could feel the way
from abandoned mill to mill:
Wainsford to Gordleton to Flexford,
coming in my mind to where
the tower, small from where I lay,
rose massively out of the land.
It wasn't a place for hermit or poet
to retreat to, but a life-mark,
common as the grass, and the stream
and the trees, as if there could be
no other world without it.

For My Brother David

My brother crouched in a culvert
while shrapnel rained down
on the road and on the brook.
He was a youth who dreamed
of flying and spent his days
with charts and balsa-wood models.

What did I dream of then?
At night my cot would rock
to the firing of an AA gun
in the neighbouring field.
The gunner, I was told, was
a Welshman with a fine tenor voice
who would sing in the dark.

What I truly remember
is a descent into the earth,
the smell and itch of the blanket
I was wrapped in, the whine
of mosquitoes in my ear,
and what they said
was the crump of bombs
exploding on Southampton Docks.

Once, we stood on the cinder path
where my brother had carried me,
and watched sparks
showering out of the night sky,
which he told me were a Heinkel,
shot down over Pompey.

What he dreamed of then
was to be 'one of the few',
a grown-up ruling the air,
a man flying out of the sun,
on the tail of the enemy.

Carpenter

In memory of Tony Hooker

Dear, dead brother,
how you loathed the people
you worked for, who
condescended to a 'mere' carpenter.
What did they know of the skill,
the truth of measure and level,
vice and the keen blade,
or of the virtues of timber?
How could they know
in body and soul
the expense of labour?

Was this why you spurned England,
turning your back on Oxford
and Henley-on-Thames?
German became your language.
But you continued to read
and re-read Thomas Hardy,
in English and in German,
anxious to identify the house
in streets you knew, where
Jude spoke his last bitter words.

The Oxford you introduced me to
was no privileged enclave,
but pubs where you drank with mates
off building sites, Irish navvies,
men with whom you laboured
on the very matter of society – you,

King's Scout to Communist,
with the looks of young Brando,
a man who loved Verdi, and Brecht,
and read the works of Gorki and Lenin.

When I was little, I worshipped you.
Later, we were comrades,
wearing out our shoes on the road
from Aldermaston to London.
Once you saved my life,
when I crept out of the house,
leaving on my pillow
a scribble that meant to say
'Gone to see the world' –
an adventure that ended
in an ammunition dump,
where you found me.
I never forgot, however much
I grew up to reject your dogma.

We became familiar strangers,
but the line remained unbroken –
knowledge in the blood
that scarecrow words cannot speak.
What we call memory is a power
that sweeps through us
like a tsunami, leaving
flotsam of time and place,
a few things saved from the wreckage.

Dear brother, I will not claim that I knew you,
for all the salvage of recollection.

Yet, how alike we must have been.
When your voice sounds in my ear
it might be my own voice that I hear.

133a, St Mary's Street
Southampton, c. 1965
for Vicky,
and in memory of John Haynes and Lorelei Farmer

Those were my psychosomatic days
chain-smoking
agonizing over *The Orators*
to the cries of vendors in Kingsland Market

Shabby street
between dockland
and gasometers of Northam
An address
approached from waste ground
up a shaking fire escape

We loved our room, Vicky
upstairs from John and Lorelei
in that slum in which we made our home
where we met to discuss
Sylvia Plath and Keith Douglas
and our own poems
                        itching to break free

Where the street ended
water soiled with industry
and smelling of salt
slopped on stones
and trading ships rode the tide
incoming
            outgoing
to a pulsing world

What a time it was between one war
still visible in damaged buildings
and the last
        coming war
                vibrant in the air.
Somehow
        beyond reason
as in memory I feel for the rusty rail
of the fire escape
a ghost of meaning fills
                the demolished rooms

Waters of Wight

Lapping waves of shingle
breaking ceaselessly
shining
or muffled in fog
for ever rounding the island
shaping and reshaping
shore and cliff and rock
exposing the leavings
of other ages
whittling bone and stone
storming or still
with countless moods
and shades of light and dark
beyond words
familiar, unknown waters
pleasuring and breaking the heart

Singing the Needles

1

It was a melancholy song,
the sound from the Needles' light
moaning through the bedroom window
on a morning of mist or fog.
It came in with the thought of wrecks,
HMS Assurance and other ships.

Three stacks, and one lost to a storm,
Lot's wife, in the eighteenth century –
she shoudn't have looked back,
gesturing to Old Harry across the Bay.

2

There are objects that stand out
with the nakedness
of being, answerable
to no one and no thing.
But these may be loved,
and mark time in the deep
of a human life – storm-battered,
or jutting out of the calm sea,
that is silver or gold in the sun.

3

Vanishing in mist, or with a sharp,
bright edge, as though, ingrained
in rock, a whole life becomes visible,
the splintered stacks stand.
Unseen, too, they are a mystery
that makes itself known,
moaning through windows
and marking a day of mist or fog.

IoW Ferry

One day in summer, when
I was working as a deckhand
on the Farringford, a passenger
spoke to me as we leaned on the rail:
'What was your skipper doing?
Was he evading U-boats?'
(I had been at the wheel,
weaving an uncertain course
as I focused on the monument
on Tennyson Down.)

The man began to reminisce,
recalling when a Lymington
to Yarmouth ferry, ancestor
to the one we were on,
had gone to the rescue
of troops from Dunkirk.

As he spoke, the Solent seemed
to become a bloody channel
and I thought how peaceful
it was on misty dawns
and on the last crossing of the day,
crawling down the Lymington River
between rows of gently rocking yachts,
when I would stand on the deck
alone, quietly repeating to myself
'Sunset and evening star...'

The Road to Keyhaven

1

Shall I call it pleasure?
The word's too weak.
        My father
would have been immersed,
paint and palette knife
at his finger-tips, body
bent forward, like a sprinter
about to start a race,
but held, as the day
flows into his eyes.

I remember him saying:
'An artist's work is his health',
this man, sometimes
tortured by nerves, who loved
nature in a tranquil mood.

2

In this painting, the sea
is out of sight, but may be felt,
between the white farmhouse
and the Island's blue
whaleback tump.
You know the sea will be still.

There are no human figures
in the painting, no one
to disturb his concentration.
Yet he would forgive me,
I know, if I intrude,
a boy with a fishing rod
tied to the cross bar of his bike
who cycles down the road
that leads gently to Keyhaven.

As I pass the white farmhouse
I am not at peace, but almost
sick with anticipation, when
the island, the blue island
first rises into sight.

Salterns

1

A cloud of steam filled
the boiling house;
salt impregnated the air;
roads all around were
black with coal ashes
from the furnaces
incessantly burning.

2

Below the seawall,
when the tide was out,
we dug in the mud for ragworm.
Behind the wall, a memory
of water diverted into tidal trenches,
solutions of brine, and an industry
that produced riches for some
by preserving fish, meat and vegetables
and worked others to death.

3

In old times, the Salterns ran
from Lymington to Hurst spit.
I loved them best at Pennington Marshes
when I was walking with my friend

and a salt wind off the Solent
was blowing fresh air into our faces.

It was somewhere that I always expected
the otherworldly to reveal itself.
My Catholic friend suspected idolatry.
'There's no special place,' he cautioned.
'Every place is special, because God is everywhere'.
I have not forgotten, and when I return
to the Salterns now, in memory,
I think of his words
and my dead friend walks with me.

Two Young Women on Milford Beach

for Sylvia
and in memory of Vivienne

1

This is a defining moment,
though we may only guess the year
from a fading print.
                        It is the shapes only
that stand out,
with the sea behind them,
                        calm on this day,
sky with a suggestion of cloud
and pebbles under their feet.

What is there to speak of future
in these silhouettes? Only a viewer
cursed or blessed with knowledge
may think he knows.

2

I too have stood in that place,
and walked on the beach
 with one of the sisters,
hand in hand, on a day
of sea and sky
that seemed like paradise.

With the wash of time,
I have returned there to grieve.

On this lost day
there is everything to hope for.

It is only a moment,
but the women stand
as if forever at the edge
of their lives, in a world
that is coming into definition
with a horizon that cannot be seen.

Under Hordle Cliffs

Remembering J. E.

1

What is one love
on the shore
of an ancient, passionate sea
making and breaking on shingle
for thousands of years?

2

Homes on the clifftop
fall down onto the beach,
and bricks lie with pebbles,
and lupins flower among shale.

Slides of blue clay preserve
traces of extinct creation
and only sandmartins
return to live there now.

3

What is one love
in a place where countless lovers
have walked in ecstasy
or grief, hearing in the hiss
of retreating waves
a noise that sounds like *loss, loss*?

Everything here is a music
that drifts and shifts, unless,
perhaps, a living moment stands
like a breakwater against the tides.

Wessex Chalkland

From the first, I was enchanted,
whether by a roadside
eruption of the white stone,
or by rounded hills like giant foreheads.
And there, at Cerne Abbas,
was an archetypal Man of Chalk,
a comic figure of lust and aggression
bound to the earth that mothered him.

Later, I learnt this was a poet's country:
Richard Jefferies' Wiltshire
and Thomas Hardy's Wessex.
Edward Thomas had left
his footprint on every path.
What word could I add
to a land so loved, where the dead,
it seemed, had breathed all the air?

But life compels one to speak
by what it brings to each of us.
On Hambledon Hill I found restoration
in a broken time. On the high downs
I picked up fossils that remembered
forgotten seas. I learnt to exist
in the company of the ancient dead.
Once more, the land was alive
with White Horses that were things of wonder –
stretched out in full gallop, or as still
as the hills they were part of.
Paths, after rain, were rivers of milk.

At Avebury, I learnt the story
of Death, from skeletons
like bones of the earth itself,
remains of makers of beaker and bowl
which showed the hands that had made them.

And all was shapely, like the barrows,
and Silbury Hill, echoing
the curves and hollows of the land.
What could be alien to us here,
in a landscape marked by the work
of human hands? Yet, what remained
was an absence, a vanishing,
a language without words, except
the speech of henge and standing stones.
If there were aliens, they were
ourselves, curious beings
who came to look and to wonder,
people who, from the silence
greeting us, recognise
that it is we, too, who are strange.

New Forest Poem

1

Purkis, the charcoal burner,
passed this way, his cart
burdened with a royal corpse.
Country people saw visions
that day. Blood cried out
from the roots of an oak.

2

Drifts of leaves.
Antlers, which might be branches,
among the trees.
A stranger could lose himself here,
panicking, as he stumbles,
bruised and scratched,
hair caught like Absalom's on thorns.

3

A Scots pine on the heath
bends to the shape of a sea wind.
An adder sunning on a tumulus
might be dreaming of Eve.

Brusher Mills, a man
my grandfather knew,

collected adders, and sold them
for scientific research. He lies
in the churchyard at Brockenhurst,
his name adorning a pub – a man
less forgotten than Marauders
and Lightnings on wartime airfields
where gorse breaks through
and ponies browse the runways.

4

I knew first love here,
in torment and in ecstasy,
with feeling that burns like fire
and leaves an after-glow
that lasts life-long
and lights up the simplest thing.

Now I can no longer visit
names retain the magic:
Sloden at dusk, Queens Bower,
Vinney Ridge, Latchmoor, Marlpit Oak.

5

I do not claim this was my first world.
But if, in thought, it proves my last,
I hope to lose myself
among the depth of trees,
feeling leafmould under my feet
and giving myself to the welcome dark.

The Knightwood Oak

They call it
'a living monument' –
five hundred years
of solid oak, which has outlived
Mary Rose and *Agamemnon*
and all the wooden walls of Buckler's Hard.
Galumphing iron-clad warriors
hoisted onto horseback
will have witnessed it.
Children, woken terrified
by a dream of nuclear holocaust,
will marvel at its strength and girth.
And if it could speak
about the monuments of time
what would it say but one word: 'acorn'?

Hatchet Pond

Mesmerised, the angler
stares at the water, imagining
something moving in the depths.
His scalp tingles at the thought
that the pond is bottomless,
the far bank haunted
by the ghost of a German pilot,
shot down over the airfield
close by, which is now a furzy waste.
A group of Scots pines across the pond
darkens as the light fades.
Only the moon is a sort
of companion, a white face
reflected in the water,
an image that wavers
with the ripples
and decomposes, and forms again.

Ghost of an unwritten poem

It wasn't one that escaped
        a solitary phantom
appearing and disappearing
among the trees

It was more like the trees themselves
or a thing like a tree
more underground than in the air
        a spirit of all the trees
no spectre, but a net
gathering invisible fungal threads
and ghostly entanglements
of roots & leaves & branches

Or else it was a being
with countless eyes of light
        beyond all human vision
though home to the smallest speck
of life.
        Or maybe it will appear
in human form – a mighty hunter
who gathers in all creatures
    bacteria

            lichen

                    spore

                        bird

                            stag

and histories

            stories

                    myths

wild wood rumours
    tales of ancient plantations
charcoal burners
               Romanies
huntsmen smashing the green
entangled coverts
blood at the roots of an oak

Imagine this thing moving
with creaking limbs
scattering acorns
which grow crossbeams
and wooden navies

It exists and does not exist
in limbo
corpse or embryo
a smoke wisp spiralling
from the compost
of a life   this haunting
may have been a dream
    a ghost
that passed through
like a storm wind
leaving vestiges
of root & branch & twig

In Praise of the Lymington River

for Terry Gifford

1

My heart-beat quickens
early on an April morning,
under oaks, walking
among windflowers
by the river, between
Balmer Lawn and Queens Bower,
as a brown trout rises.

2

How many moods have I known
by this river between forest headwaters
and reedbeds and Solent waters
where it loses itself and is renewed?

A February day when I cried with cold
but went on casting with numbed hands
or a summer evening of mayfly hatch,
ripples under alders on the far bank
where my greased line snaked.
A run of seatrout, shoals breaking the surface.

3

What I would recall now
is simply the touch of it,
this river, which isn't mighty,
gathering tributaries as it flows
and tidal as far as the Shallows
and even Boldre Bridge,
mixing salt and fresh water,
and with an occasional flatfish
among dace and seatrout.

4

Sit still, listen, watch
and life comes to you.
A mouse appears, attracted
by crumbs from your sandwich.
Is that wave among waves an otter
as it swims downstream?
A flash of colour, gone in a blink
as a kingfisher arrows past.
On the bank, a rabbit cries,
frozen in the gaze of a stoat.

5

Once, upstream at Highland Water,
river in spate a brown turbulence,
and acorns dropping in, explosively,

I stood wretched on the bank,
feeling no ground under my feet,
and what I saw and felt restored me,
so that life flowed out into the world.

Two Brothers

for Peter Larkin

Brother Oswald

I was a poor pupil, dreaming
 in his French class of a certain girl.
But he was kind to me,
and kind to everyone,
and gentle to the bulldog,
poor slobbering Chester,
everyone else despised
or was afraid of,
that followed him about
adoringly, and licked his hand.
I did not know him well
but learnt he had been a soldier
in the war, and brave.
He was a man of great heart
who died in the faith.
When I dream of him
he smiles forgivingly
and I am ashamed of my ignorance
of the language of romance.

Brother Nicholas

How well he played himself,
old Nick, with his twirl
of grey hair on his head
like a unicorn's small horn,
which he would twist
as he stood in front of us.
He loved holiness, and thought
some boys in our class,
seminarians, were saints,
which I doubted.
Yet it wasn't my scepticism
he taught me, but the qualities
of weathers, climates
and regions: different soils
and life-enabling waterways,
the grittiness of things, and all
the riches of the generative Earth.

Author and Mariner

In memory of Jonathan Raban

You were always the savvy one,
Jonathan, and talented, as I knew
when we were scarcely more than boys
and I read articles you wrote about poets
for your father's parish magazine.
We called you Oscar then – on your first step
from Pennington to London and Seattle.

Were you dreaming of America
when I woke you in the caravan
in the vicarage garden, and we cycled
to the lake at Walhampton and set up our rods
in the eery mist of a June dawn?

When coots and moorhens
broke the hush, and bubbles rose
by lily pads, and we cast out our lines
with trembling hands,
did you dream of wilder waters?

On a Sunny Day at Hurst Castle

When evangelists speak
of desiring the kingdom,
I remember a distant time
when grasshoppers spurted
from long grass at every footstep
by the castle walls and wind off the sea
seemed fresher for the butterflies
that fluttered by the water's edge.

How rich we seemed with time
in a world that accepted us,
but which we did not think we possessed.
How powerful the sun seemed,
which we had not harnessed.
It was easy to believe in the kindness of God
and to desire only what we had
with grasshoppers at our feet, leaping and leaping.

A Man of Heyshott

for James Simpson

He is familiar
with the Bee Orchid
and the Chalkhill Blue.
Badgers and owls
are his neighbours –
alive in his poems
but not domesticated –
wild beings that share
the life of the Sussex parish.

He is a man for far views
who climbs Heyshott Down
to the hummocky summit
where overgrown chalk pits
show the labour of another age.
Out of breath, he returns
to his desk, a poet
who seeks words for the owl,
the badger and the Bee Orchid
and for love of their land.

A Lost Painting

1

Sunflower in a watering can,
the flower face glowing
against the metal
in a late summer sun.
You can feel the hand that placed it there,
see with the measuring eye,
taste a pleasure
in this homely object,
something so simple
which brings a world to a focus.

2

We can imagine the painter's hand
brushing the canvas, see him
standing back, squeezing paints from tubes.
It is an everyday thing he loves –
a sunflower,
             a watering can,
objects drawn together
which catch the late summer sun.

3

What they show
is the man's hand
and the soil he loved to work,
the thirsty, nurturing earth.
This radiant conjunction
calls back a life busy with growing things,
and the quiet of a long sun-warmed hour
of contemplation.

4

It is something lost
that I speak of – a canvas,
gone from a home
that no longer exists – a painting
that may hang on a stranger's wall,
providing another with an image
that holds the eye, the glow
of a flower face against metal
in late summer sun.
And perhaps it is all that remains,
the one solid thing
of a world of memory,
some home-thought
for a stranger to enjoy.

5

It was his moment –
we can be sure of that –
it belonged to him,
the painter, the gardener,
the man relishing the warmth,
the colours of a late summer day,
a hint of autumn
in the smell of apples
and of garden soil.
It would not be like this
for ever, but there they were –
sunflower
            watering can –
in place together,
one thing
vibrant with being
at the edge of time.

Artist on Chesil Beach

for Jenny Hunt

Chert by flint, pebble
knocking on pebble,
percussion, grinding
and always the musical
swash swash swash
of waves sluicing
gently or storm-driven,
lashing a white dragon tail.

*

This is the place she comes to,
sun-struck or in squall-
flung spume, where she makes
a poem or a sketch, ordering
what looks like chaos,
but observes an order of its own:
laws of sun and moon, sources
of tales we tell, fables
in which jaws of the tide
spit up shingle and salt waves
shift the waves of stone.

*

What a world of things:
images the blind maker
creates and destroys,
changes and preserves:

quartzite by blood-stone
bivalve and gastropod
chalcedony, destination
of the pilgrim scallop shell,
the urchin flowering in stone.

*

Gulls hanging on the air,
tern shining as it dives
knifing the water,
a feather plucked from a wing
drifting with the tide.
A salty fishy smell of time.
Waves on waves, continually
make and unmake, breaking on the shore.

*

Immersion is what the poet
placing herself desires,
the artist with sketchbook
and words, walker
on chalk pebbles, flint,
kelp and dried wrack,
observing this very now
the breadth and breath
of it, sand wraith
and stony promontory,
stepping on the rim
of this oldest, freshest world.

Beach Canvas

for Frances Hatch

1

She is open to the open air –
a painter kneeling
on bonfire-blackened shingle
mixed with debris the sea has tossed up.

Rain won't deter her.
Quite the contrary;
it too will be something to hand,
softening surfaces, seeping in.

She works with stuff
that is all a meeting and a mixing:
greensand, gault, blue lias
this present moment
with geological ages
on the Jurassic coast.

Paint encounters earth
fallen from cliffs,
plant life, flotsam, all
the material makings of place.

2

As she anchors her canvas
with a rock and light flashes

where the cliff torn with a fall
catches the sun, I want to tell her
what her art means to me.
I could put it simply
and it would be true.
What she brings me into,
quickened with imagination,
is the living world.

But is that enough?

 We need words that glow with inner light:
words that come with a touch
of life that makes them what they are –
life of flesh and spirit,
and not with colour daubed on,
but with the inner glow
that is energy,
the vibrant flower
        and the mud it grows in.

What she reveals,
what I seek to speak of,
is place renewed,
broken shore and wave breaking
here, at this moment, all the instability
of the land we live on and love.

Gull Dying

1

Gull with a broken wing
flapping in the tide
that ebbs and flows ceaselessly
lifting the bird's stiff wings
rocking the feathers
entangled in weed.

All is movement,
        rhythms of day and night
light and dark streaming
with energy, birds
screaming and swooping
under the flying cloud.

Vacancy will come
but for now
all the world is wings
to the dying eye.

2

We can do nothing
to help, an old woman
and a disabled man
who pick our way
among the shingle,
looking down for signs

of ancient life, where fossils
lie among the flints,
looking up as a cruise ship
passes down the channel,
thinking briefly of them,
travellers and far places,
the wide ocean and the globe
while the gull flounders
calling our attention back
as waves break, and break again
and the tide working
against the flapping wings
takes it slowly out to sea.

The Bridge (2)

Stone bridge
that has carried over
generations
                standing
where the stream slips by
and creates
                underneath
an illusion of stillness
green-shadowed
where the ancient
cannibal trout lives
a terror to little fish
where a boy stares
under stone arch
hypnotized   standing
where memory streams
for an old man
snagging moments
                ripples
eyes of light
                dissolving
as dark returns
where he watches
beside himself
with expectation
in love with time

Silent Companion

Invisible One,
how you have walked with me
on a hard road.
Dare I call you Lord?
Whoever you are,
permit me to speak to you,
not with knowledge,
but unknowing, and with love
of your understanding,
felt but not seen – you
who hold in your heart
the poor self in turmoil,
the wretched I-alone
that reaches out with theadbare words.

I recall ways you have gone with me,
through paths by prickly gorse
and golden flowers, by streams
in sunlight and in shadow, under trees
that were winter-bare or in leaf or blossom
and above all, threading
terrible rooms, ordinarily
full of alien faces, floor like the deck
of a trawler in a heaving sea.

Time, then, on the brightest day
was a small, dark cell
in the prison of the self,
and without you, though
you cannot be seen,

I was struck dumb,
a figure in a picture
like the judgement of the damned.

What can I say of you, Spirit?
What word can bring you
like a parable into the meaning
of a common day? I have nothing
but the language of need,
and an intuition, a feeling
that, since I was a boy, you have walked with me
on hard roads, invisible,
but sharing the terror of my human world.

Walking in Longleat Woods

Now the bluebells are fading,
will we hear a cuckoo?
Other birds dart around us
anxious about their young.
We startle a deer, which bounds away,
crashing through undergrowth.
A pheasant squawks raucously.
Fear seems to follow our every step.

You tell me about the devil
that squats on your shoulder.
Vile tempter. How can I help you
to shake him off? Words are so weak.
We plan our 'book', which may save you.

I kick a log and you tell me it's a man's act
asserting himself. No, I say, it is simple
appreciation of the solidity of the thing.
On such a day, with life running
in the veins of leaves and flowing
through every sentient being
how can we bear to be
such passionate reasoners,
debating how we may outwit death?

Revenant

I feel for the latch in my mind.
But I do not need to open the door.
Memory leads me in,
where I find each room by touch
and climb the stairs.
All is familiar, and everything has changed.

'You will be the last', my mother said.
She, too, remembered the emptiness,
seeing her whole family round a table
dining together – father, sisters, brother
and her dead mother held in their hearts.

She, too, knew that old age
is the beloved house we return to
where nobody is at home.

Leaf

First on the oak, with a colour
that some call green,
and I have found, year
after year, indescribable.

It does not matter
that I may not see another
next year, wonderingly.
Only let another leaf come,
fresh, moist, and beyond words.

Acknowledgements

Some of these poems, in some cases in earlier versions, appeared in the following publications, to whose editors I wish to express my gratitude:

Poetry Salzburg Review
Shearsman
The Brazen Head (Australia)
Tears in the Fence
Temenos Academy Review
Times Literary Supplement

'A lost painting' and 'The road to Keyhaven' first appeared in *Alive with Sunlight & Shadow* (with Aubrey Hooker), Actaeon Press, 2022.

'Salterns' and 'Under Hordle Cliffs' are radical reworkings of poems from *Solent Shore* (Manchester: Carcanet Press, 1978).

A note on autobiographical poetry

Preludes are primarily autobiographical poems written in old age. I was born and brought up on the south coast, near Southampton and between the New Forest and the Solent. This is the principal ground of this book.

Age, I have found, brings pressure to write out of one's life, to recover shaping experiences, and to express gratitude for what has been given. Inevitably, one of the principal themes of this book is the making of a poet. This may seem to sit oddly with what in a poem in *Solent Shore* (1978) I called 'the sludge of nostalgia'. I distrust the autobiographical impulse with its temptation to egotism and assumptions of finality. Poetry, like the life that engenders it, is a process, each poem, one hopes, a step towards expression and meaning. My early idea of nostalgia came with a horror of being stuck in an idealized version of the past. Much later, in another poem, I realized that nostalgia, in releasing memory, can be an energy.

In a long life, I have stumbled on key words. One is *quickness*, which I found in Henry Vaughan's poem of that name, and have adapted for my own sense of livingness, and the otherness of reality, that which words can only point to. Another key word, which I came on in writing poems in this book, is *immersion*. It is the act of being completely self-given, as in my father painting and in his gardening, and in the life of the artist on Chesil Beach 'trying to catch the life around'. It implies a close relationship to place. Places make us, and we create with their materials, whether negatively or positively. The conviction that every place is a centre of being has characterized my work from the beginning. In exploring the terrain of memory, I have sought to make it live as it does in me, but also as it lives beyond me, not as in the weak word *environment*, but in the one life we share with all beings in an animate universe.

Milton Keynes UK
Ingram Content Group UK Ltd.
UKHW041810250624
444687UK00001B/71